America the Beautiful
In the words of
WALT WHITMAN

This memorial to a Civil War regiment stands in Gettysburg National Park.
Whitman questioned whether the cause justified the death of so many young Americans.

AMERICA THE BEAUTIFUL
In the words of

Walt Whitman

by the Editors of COUNTRY BEAUTIFUL
Editorial Direction: Michael P. Dineen
Edited by Robert L. Polley

Published by Country Beautiful Corporation

COUNTRY BEAUTIFUL: *Publisher and Editorial Director:* Michael P. Dineen; *Executive Editor:* Robert L. Polley; *Senior Editors:* Kenneth L. Schmitz, James H. Robb; *Associate Art Directors:* Wilbur Howe, Mitchel L. Heinrichs; *Photography:* Douglas C. Green; *Editorial Assistants:* Carolyn Muchhala, Lawrence Kenney, Janice M. Puta; *Executive Director, Sales and Marketing:* Richard W. Stone; *Production:* John Dineen; *Circulation Manager:* Trudy Schnittka; *Administrative Secretary:* Donna Griesemer; *Editorial Secretary:* Christine Maynard

Country Beautiful Corporation is a division of Flick-Reedy Corporation: *President:* Frank Flick; *Vice President and General Manager:* Michael P. Dineen; *Treasurer and Secretary:* Bok Robertson.

CONTENTS

COME, said my Soul,
Such verses for my Body let us write, (for we are one,)
That should I after death invisibly return,
Or, long, long hence, in other spheres,
There to some group of mates the chants resuming,
(Tallying Earth's soil, trees, winds, tumultuous waves,)
Ever with pleas'd smile I may keep on,
Ever and ever yet the verses owning—as, first, I here and now,
Signing for Soul and Body, set to them my name,

Walt Whitman

INTRODUCTION

The writings of Walt Whitman are the extraordinary work of an artist unique for his time and place and extremely uncommon in any culture or era. Until the late 1840's, when he was nearly thirty years old, he was a writer of competent journalism, shallow stories, and banal, imitative poetry. Yet within ten years, Ralph Waldo Emerson hailed him as author of *the* American poem. Today he is considered the most influential and relevant of all nineteenth-century American poets.

Although such phenomena can never be fully understood, the decades preceding the flowering of Whitman's genius were years of absorbing preparation. For, to a remarkable extent, Whitman's character and talent were shaped by his family and the physical environment in which he grew up and by the most dynamic social and political forces at work in the nation during the period when he approached maturity. Enriched by growing experience, he gradually and consciously embraced these forces and developed a bold new language and style which seemed particularly well adapted to giving poetic expression to them. His genius for absorption—stimulated by the pressures of his ambition and his poetic sensibility—became a genius for creativity.

Whitman was born in 1819 in the little farming community of West Hills, Long Island, of Dutch and Yankee, Quaker and Calvinist ancestry. The Whitman family estates had once been extensive but they had diminished to very little. Whitman's father was a carpenter who liked to sleep, as he said, on floors of his own making and he was a friend of Tom Paine, author of *Common Sense*, which hastened the Declaration of Independence. The family had fiercely supported the American Revolution and they were Democrats when to be a Democrat meant to vote for the rights of man against the vested interests. During these years of America's westward expansion, an expansion that persisted throughout Whitman's life, the democracy espoused by the Democratic Party was at its most vigorous and aspiring.

Around Walt's fifth birthday he moved with his family to Brooklyn, but he returned many times to the still unblemished countryside of Long Island where he called the birds and flowers by name, to the villages on the bays and the inland hamlets he knew well, and to the beaches where he said he learned to write his poetry by shouting Homer to the sounds of the sea gulls and the waves beating upon the shore. It was from his experiences on the island that he formulated his central ideas, his philosophy of nature, his individualism, his belief in social democracy and his loving admiration for "powerful uneducated persons," such as his mother who knew how to mount a horse and till a field.

But if he was always "Starting from Paumanok"—the name the Indians gave to fish-shaped Long Island—he was also "Crossing Brooklyn Ferry" again and again. One road led Whitman from Brooklyn, then little more than a small town, back to the land of rural Long Island. The other road took him to urban America as manifested by "stately . . . mast-hemm'd Manhattan," where he completed his training as a printer at the age of sixteen, after a three- or four-year apprenticeship in Brooklyn. New York, already a metropolis, was an impressive symbol of turbulent, expansive America. Although art and literature here were still primarily pale reflections of Old World models, the city displayed the energies of burgeoning trade, transportation and industry and the optimism of thousands of immigrants who entered the continent on their way west. Whitman was fascinated by the throngs on New York streets, preferring the workmen and farmers to the complacent and static elements in American society.

All of this—"whatever I touch, or am touched from"— he identified himself with to an extreme degree. "Remember, the book *Leaves of Grass* arose," he told a friend many years later, "out of my life in Brooklyn and New York . . . absorbing a million people, for fifteen years, with an intimacy, an eagerness, an abandon, probably never equalled."

It was during these years that Whitman educated himself. In Brooklyn he had attended public school for about six years as an apparently indifferent student. His father worked hard at his carpenter's trade but could not support his growing family so the boys had to become self-supporting at an early age. One of his first jobs was as an office boy

The elderly Whitman as he was portrayed by Thomas Eakins.

for a law firm where his employer helped him with handwriting and composition and subscribed for Whitman to a circulating library, the beginning of his real education. Whitman became a voracious reader and the range of his reading was great, but eventually he became more discriminating, focusing his attention on the potentialities of the common man and his "long journey" toward personal freedom and full self-development. His feeling for words was enhanced—like Benjamin Franklin before him and William Dean Howells and Mark Twain after—by his training as a printer. Before he finished his apprenticeship Whitman was contributing "sentimental bits" to a Long Island newspaper.

In 1835, soon after he became a full-fledged printer, an economic depression in New York City caused Whitman to begin teaching school on Long Island, which he described as "one of my best experiences." For the next fourteen years he used his abilities to advantage while serving in a number of teaching positions and working on a succession of newspapers, sometimes as editor. He also became increasingly involved in politics, electioneering for President Van Buren in his unsuccessful campaign for a second term in 1840. He lost his most prestigious job as editor of the *Brooklyn Daily Eagle* in 1848 because of his vociferous opposition to the extension of slavery into annexed territories. That same year a journey to New Orleans and back by way of the Mississippi, Great Lakes and Hudson River showed him much more of the country than he had ever seen before.

About 1845 Whitman's father began a physical decline which required Whitman to begin contributing financially to his family. After a paper he was editing folded in 1849 he had to find other means of income. During the next five years he supported his family adequately, mainly through his activities as a building contractor and land speculator, and he had enough money left over for a few luxuries. However, Whitman then turned away from this kind of life.

Sometime before 1847, when his journalistic prose had reached a level of fully effective expression, he began experimenting in notebooks with poetry of a completely unconventional kind. Transcendental in tone, rhythmic without being metrical, this was the beginning of a new mode of expression which Whitman spent the remainder of his life trying to perfect.

The poetry of Whitman's time had become dominated by conventionalized sentiment and romanticized morality and was restricted to a few metrical styles which encouraged shallow thinking and feeling, "copious dribble" Whitman called it. Whitman had written some of this himself and the critical influence which encouraged him to search for new feelings and forms was Ralph Waldo Emerson, one of the most respected literary men of his day. In an essay, "The Poet," published in 1844, Emerson wrote:

> We have yet had no genius in America, with tyrannous eye, which knew the value of our incomparable materials, and saw, in the barbarism and materialism of the times, another carnival of the same gods whose picture he so much admires in Homer. . . . Banks and tariffs, the newspaper and caucus . . . are flat and dull to dull people, but rest on the same foundations of wonder as the town of Troy and the temple of Delphi. . . . Our log-rolling, our stumps and their politics, our fisheries, our Negroes and Indians . . . the northern trade, the southern planting, the western clearing, Oregon and Texas, are yet unsung. Yet America is a poem in our eyes; its ample geography dazzles the imagination, and it will not wait long for metres.

This catalogue of materials and this grand purpose seem to have ignited Whitman. Later he said that he had been "simmering" and Emerson had brought him "to a boil."

9

In July 1855, eleven years after Emerson's essay, a strange looking book appeared in New York. This thin quarto of ninety-five pages, entitled *Leaves of Grass,* was bound in green cloth and stamped with floral designs, the gold lettering of the title sprouting roots and foliage in many directions. No author's name appeared on the title page but the first long, untitled poem (later to be called "Song of Myself") contained the lines: "Walt Whitman, an American, one of the roughs, a kosmos,/Disorderly, fleshy and sensual . . . eating, drinking and breeding." The language and poetical structure of the book seemed even more eccentric than its physical appearance. The preface, probably the most famous document in American literary history, was a manifesto which proudly proclaimed that here finally was a poet worthy of the strength and spaciousness of the United States, which "themselves are essentially the greatest poem." This first edition did not sell well but Whitman sent a copy to Emerson who replied with a letter stating: "I find it the most extraordinary piece of wit and wisdom that America has yet contributed."

It was Whitman's intention from the beginning that *Leaves of Grass* should grow the way a man or a nation grows. He devoted virtually the remainder of his life to enlarging and continually revising this volume of which he said, "This is no book, /Who touches this touches a man. . . ." During the following decades he supported himself as best he could by working as a newspaper correspondent, secretary and government clerk in Washington, D. C. After he was struck by paralysis in 1873 he was unable to work and lived with his brother in Camden, New Jersey. The proofs of the last edition of *Leaves of Grass* passed through his hands only a few months before he died in 1892. Until this century Whitman was never admired as much in this country as he was in England, although his death was the occasion for public praise.

Walt Whitman's birthplace near Huntington, Long Island.

Whitman once said that "I sometimes think *Leaves* is only a language experiment," and his contribution toward the recognition of American English as a distinct and vital entity is well recognized. Whitman was capable of noisy rhetoric and lyrical diffuseness, but he deserves to be judged by his best work. He understood that language was not simply abstract constructions but that it had arisen out of the needs and joys and struggles of long generations of humanity. The freedom of his rhythmic line, which has had considerable influence on modern poetry, was based on his rediscovery of an old principle of English speech, for the rhythm of Anglo-Saxon poetry was based on the natural fall of the accents rather than the strict distribution of syllables.

This aspect of Whitman's work, however, is secondary to what he tried to say. "No one will get at my verses who insists on viewing them as a literary performance." His main themes were love—both physical and spirtual, for he thought these inseparable and mutually beneficial—and democracy, not to be defined as majority rule, which may become tyrannical, but as the possibility for the fullest degree of individual self-development. Because Whitman believed that love in its various manifestations was the law of nature and that "as the greatest lessons of Nature through the universe are perhaps the lessons of variety and freedom," he felt that New World democracy—which embodies love as the key to individual and social behavior and which allows the greatest diversity and freedom—had a special destiny in this New World of untrammeled natural abundance and seemingly limitless space. Even the chaos, corruption, and self-seeking he saw in Washington during the Civil War could not dissuade him. "For America . . . counts, as I reckon, for her justification and success, . . . almost entirely on the future."

But more than reinvigorated language and an intellectual commitment to noble themes is needed to explain the sources of Whitman's expressive power. It is based on the intensity of his feeling ("I do not ask a wounded person how he feels . . . I myself become the wounded person, . . .) and the scope of his vision, ranging from the smallest particle, the atom ("For every atom belonging to me as good belongs to you") and one of the commonest things, grass ("A child said *What is the grass?*") to the cosmic level in both time (". . . whether I come to my own today or in ten thousand or ten million years, /I can cheerfully take it now, . . . or I can wait.") and space ("Smile O voluptuous coolbreathed earth!). It was this power, usually stated in personal terms, which enabled Whitman to express to the fullest extent the American belief in the sacredness of self and thus to become the "poet of democracy" he described in his 1855 preface as one whose "country absorbs him as affectionately as he has absorbed it."

—Robert L. Polley

Winslow Homer, *Gathering Autumn Leaves*, 1873

I

The Poet Awakens
in the Boy

Through the song of a mockingbird, the poet was awakened in Whitman.

OUT OF THE CRADLE ENDLESSLY ROCKING

Out of the cradle endlessly rocking,
Out of the mocking-bird's throat, the musical shuttle,
Out of the Ninth-month midnight,
Over the sterile sands and the fields beyond, where the child
    leaving his bed wander'd alone, bareheaded, barefoot,
Down from the shower'd halo,
Up from the mystic play of shadows twining and twisting as
    if they were alive,
Out from the patches of briers and blackberries,
From the memories of the bird that chanted to me,

From the memories of a bird, I, a chanter of pains and joys, this reminiscence sing . . .

From your memories sad brother, from the fitful risings and
  fallings I heard,
From under that yellow half-moon late-risen and swollen as
  if with tears,
From those beginning notes of yearning and love there in
  the mist,
From the thousand responses of my heart never to cease,
From the myriad thence-arous'd words,
From the word stronger and more delicious than any,
From such as now they start the scene revisiting,
As a flock, twittering, rising, or overhead passing,
Borne hither, ere all eludes me, hurriedly,
A man, yet by these tears a little boy again,
Throwing myself on the sand, confronting the waves,
I, chanter of pains and joys, uniter of here and hereafter,
Taking all hints to use them, but swiftly leaping beyond
  them,
A reminiscence sing.

Once Paumanok,
When the lilac-scent was in the air and Fifth-month grass
  was growing,
Up this seashore in some briers,
Two feather'd guests from Alabama, two together,
And their nest, and four light-green eggs spotted with brown,
And every day the he-bird to and fro near at hand,
And every day the she-bird crouch'd on her nest, silent, with
  bright eyes,
And every day I, a curious boy, never too close, never
  disturbing them,
Cautiously peering, absorbing, translating.

*Whitman listened, absorbed and strove to
translate the diverse voices of nature.*

Algimantas Kezys, S.J.

Day come white, or night come black
we two keep together . . .

Shine! shine! shine!
Pour down your warmth, great sun!
While we bask, we two together.

Two together!
Winds blow south, or winds blow north,
Day come white, or night come black,
Home, or rivers and mountains from home,
Singing all time, minding no time,
While we two keep together.

Till of a sudden,
May-be kill'd, unknown to her mate,
One forenoon the she-bird crouch'd not on the nest,
Nor return'd that afternoon, nor the next,
Nor ever appear'd again.

And thenceforward all summer in the sound of the sea,
And at night under the full of the moon in calmer weather,
Over the hoarse surging of the sea,
Or flitting from brier to brier by day,
I saw, I heard at intervals the remaining one, the he-bird,
The solitary guest from Alabama.

Blow! blow! blow!
Blow up sea-winds along Paumanok's shore;
I wait and I wait till you blow my mate to me.

Yes, when the stars glisten'd,
All night long on the prong of a moss-scallop'd stake,
Down almost amid the slapping waves,
Sat the lone singer wonderful causing tears.

He call'd on his mate,
He pour'd forth the meanings which I of all men know.

Yes my brother I know,
The rest might not, but I have treasur'd every note,
For more than once dimly down to the beach gliding,
Silent, avoiding the moonbeams, blending myself with the
    shadows,
Recalling now the obscure shapes, the echoes, the sounds
    and sights after their sorts,
The white arms out in the breakers tirelessly tossing,
I, with bare feet, a child, the wind wafting my hair,
Listen'd long and long.

Opposite: Time is stilled while the lovers are together.

Under the full of the moon, the boy listens
for the notes of the she-bird.

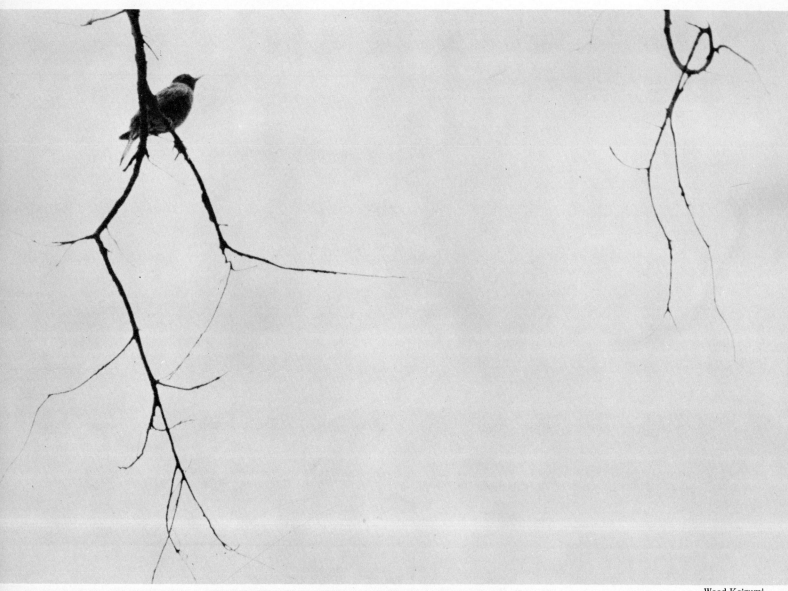

And the lonely he-bird yearns for his mate's return.

Wood Koizumi

Listen'd to keep, to sing, now translating the notes,
Following you my brother.

Soothe! soothe! soothe!
Close on its wave soothes the wave behind,
And again another behind embracing and lapping, every
*   one close,*
But my love soothes not me, not me.

Low hangs the moon, it rose late,
It is lagging—O I think it is heavy with love, with love.

O madly the sea pushes upon the land,
With love, with love.

O night! do I not see my love fluttering out among the
    breakers?
What is that little black thing I see there in the white?

Loud! loud! loud!
Loud I call to you, my love!

High and clear I shoot my voice over the waves,
Surely you must know who is here, is here,
You must know who I am, my love.

Low-hanging moon!
What is that dusky spot in your brown yellow?
O it is the shape, the shape of my mate!
O moon do not keep her from me any longer.

Land! land! land!
Whichever way I turn, O I think you could give me my mate
    back again if you only would,
For I am almost sure I see her dimly whichever way I look.

O rising stars!
Perhaps the one I want so much will rise, will rise with
    some of you.

O throat! O trembling throat!
Sound clearer through the atmosphere!
Pierce the woods, the earth,
Somewhere listening to catch you must be the one I want.

Shake out carols!
Solitary here, the night's carols!
Carols of lonesome love! death's carols!
Carols under that lagging, yellow, waning moon!
O under that moon where she droops almost down into the
    sea!
O reckless despairing carols.

Do I not see my love fluttering among the breakers?
Loud! Loud! I call to thee over the waves . . .

*The approaching darkness
intensifies his desolation.*

But soft! sink low!
Soft! let me just murmur,
And do you wait a moment you husky-nois'd sea,
For somewhere I believe I heard my mate responding to me,
So faint, I must be still, be still to listen,
But not altogether still, for then she might not come
    immediately to me.

Hither my love!
Here I am! here!
With this just sustain'd note I announce myself to you,
This gentle call is for you my love, for you.

Do not be decoy'd elsewhere,
That is the whistle of the wind, it is not my voice,
That is the fluttering, the fluttering of the spray,
Those are the shadows of leaves.

O darkness! O in vain!
O I am very sick and sorrowful.

O brown halo in the sky near the moon, drooping upon
    the sea!
O troubled reflection in the sea!
O throat! O throbbing heart!
And I singing uselessly, uselessly all the night.

O past! O happy life! O songs of joy!
In the air, in the woods, over fields,
Loved! loved! loved! loved! loved!
But my mate no more, no more with me!
We two together no more.

Even the low-hanging sun mirrors the despair of the he-bird.

Demon or bird! (said the boy's soul)
for I, my tongue's use sleeping,
know now what I am for . . .

The aria sinking,
All else continuing, the stars shining,
The winds blowing, the notes of the bird continuous echoing,
With angry moans the fierce old mother incessantly moaning,
On the sands of Paumanok's shore gray and rustling,
The yellow half-moon enlarged, sagging down, drooping,
    the face of the sea almost touching,
The boy ecstatic, with his bare feet the waves, with his hair
    the atmosphere dallying,
The love in the heart long pent, now loose, now at last
    tumultuously bursting,
The aria's meaning, the ears, the soul, swiftly depositing,
The strange tears down the cheeks coursing,
The colloquy there, the trio, each uttering,
The undertone, the savage old mother incessantly crying,
To the boy's soul's questions sullenly timing, some drown'd
    secret hissing,
To the outsetting bard.

Demon or bird! (said the boy's soul,)
Is it indeed toward your mate you sing? or is it really to me?
For I, that was a child, my tongue's use sleeping, now I have
    heard you,
Now in a moment I know what I am for, I awake,
And already a thousand singers, a thousand songs, clearer,
    louder and more sorrowful than yours,
A thousand warbling echoes have started to life within me,
    never to die.

O you singer solitary, singing by yourself, projecting me,
O solitary me listening, never more shall I cease
    perpetuating you,
Never more shall I escape, never more the reverberations,
Never more the cries of unsatisfied love be absent from me,
Never again leave me to be the peaceful child I was before
    what there in the night,
By the sea under the yellow and sagging moon,
The messenger there arous'd, the fire, the sweet hell within,
The unknown want, the destiny of me.

The boy, ecstatic, awakens to the full-throated echo of love.

*And the first object he look'd upon, that object he became,
for a day, or years, or stretching cycles of years . . .*

Doug Green

*The warbling notes of the bird are fused
with sea-waves lapping wet sands.*

O give me the clew! (it lurks in the night here somewhere,)
O if I am to have so much, let me have more!

A word then, (for I will conquer it,)
The word final, superior to all,
Subtle, sent up—what is it?—I listen;
Are you whispering it, and have been all the time,
      you sea-waves?
Is that it from your liquid rims and wet sands?

Whereto answering, the sea,
Delaying not, hurrying not,
Whisper'd me through the night, and very plainly before
      daybreak,
Lisp'd to me the low and delicious word death,
And again, death, death, death, death,
Hissing melodies, neither like the bird nor like my arous'd
      child's heart,
But edging near as privately for me rustling at my feet,
Creeping thence steadily up to my ears and laving me softly
      all over,
Death, death, death, death, death.

Which I do not forget,
But fuse the song of my dusky demon and brother,
That he sang to me in the moonlight on Paumanok's gray
      beach,
With the thousand responsive songs at random,
My own songs awaked from that hour,
And with them the key, the word up from the waves,
The word of the sweetest song and all songs,
That strong and delicious word which, creeping to my feet,
(Or like some old crone rocking the cradle, swathed in sweet
      garments, bending aside,)
The sea whisper'd me.

22

All that the boy touched, saw or heard, became a part of his being.

THERE WAS A CHILD WENT FORTH

There was a child went forth every day,
And the first object he look'd upon, that object he became,
And that object became part of him for the day or a certain
    part of the day,
Or for many years or stretching cycles of years.

The early lilacs became part of this child,
And grass and white and red morning-glories, and white and
    red clover, and the song of the phoebe-bird,
And the Third-month lambs and the sow's pink-faint litter,
    and the mare's foal and the cow's calf,
And the noisy brood of the barnyard or by the mire of the
    pond-side,
And the fish suspending themselves so curiously below there,
    and the beautiful curious liquid,
And the water-plants with their graceful flat heads, all
    became part of him.

The village seen from afar, the light and shadow across roofs and gables, and all the changes of city and country . . .

The field-sprouts of Fourth-month and Fifth-month became
    part of him,
Winter-grain sprouts and those of the light-yellow corn, and
    the esculent roots of the garden,
And the apple-trees cover'd with blossoms and the fruit
    afterward, and wood-berries, and the commonest weeds
    by the road,
And the old drunkard staggering home from the outhouse of
    the tavern whence he had lately risen,
And the schoolmistress that pass'd on her way to the school,
And the friendly boys that pass'd, and the quarrelsome boys,
And the tidy and fresh-cheek'd girls, and the barefoot negro
    boy and girl,
And all the changes of city and country wherever he went.

His own parents, he that had father'd him and she that had
    conceiv'd him in her womb and birth'd him,
They gave this child more of themselves than that,
They gave him afterward every day, they became part of
    him.

The mother at home quietly placing the dishes on the supper-
    table,
The mother with mild words, clean her cap and gown, a
    wholesome odor falling off her person and clothes as she
    walks by,
The father, strong, self-sufficient, manly, mean, anger'd,
    unjust,
The blow, the quick loud word, the tight bargain, the crafty
    lure,
The family usages, the language, the company, the furniture,
    the yearning and swelling heart,
Affection that will not be gainsay'd, the sense of what is real,
    the thought if after all it should prove unreal,
The doubts of day-time and the doubts of night-time, the
    curious whether and how,
Whether that which appears so is so, or is it all flashes and
    specks?
Men and women crowding fast in the streets, if they are not
    flashes and specks what are they?
The streets themselves and the facades of houses, and goods
    in the windows,

The stillness of New England's countryside has changed little since Whitman's time.

Vehicles, teams, the heavy-plank'd wharves, the huge
    crossing at the ferries,
The village on the highland seen from afar at sunset, the
    river between,
Shadows, aureola and mist, the light falling on roofs and
    gables of white or brown two miles off,
The schooner near by sleepily dropping down the tide, the
    little boat slack-tow'd astern,
The hurrying tumbling waves, quick-broken crests, slapping,
The strata of color'd clouds, the long bar of maroon-tint
    away solitary by itself, the spread of purity it lies
    motionless in,
The horizon's edge, the flying sea-crow, the fragrance of salt
    marsh and shore mud,
These became part of that child who went forth every day,
    and who now goes, and will always go forth every day.

Whitman's love of life inspired him to celebrate the full spectrum of living beings, from the lowly caterpillar to the strong-breasted buffalo.

Solitary, singing in the West, aware of the
buffalo herds, the earth, rocks —
I strike out for a New World . . .

BEGINNING MY STUDIES

Beginning my studies the first step pleas'd me so much,
The mere fact consciousness, these forms, the power of
    motion,
The least insect or animal, the senses, eyesight, love,
The first step I say awed me and pleas'd me so much,
I have hardly gone and hardly wish'd to go any farther,
But stop and loiter all the time to sing it in ecstatic songs.

From STARTING FROM PAUMANOK

Starting from fish-shaped Paumanok where I was born,
Well-begotten, and rais'd by a perfect mother,
After roaming many lands, lover of populous pavements,
Dweller in Mannahatta my city, or on southern savannas,
Or a soldier camp'd or carrying my knapsack and gun, or a
    miner in California,
Or rude in my home in Dakota's woods, my diet meat, my
    drink from the spring,
Or withdrawn to muse and meditate in some deep recess,
Far from the clank of crowds intervals passing rapt and
    happy,
Aware of the fresh free giver the flowing Missouri, aware of
    mighty Niagara,
Aware of the buffalo herds grazing the plains, the hirsute
    and strong-breasted bull,
Of earth, rocks, Fifth-month flowers experienced, stars, rain,
    snow, my amaze,
Having studied the mocking-bird's tones and the flight of the
    mountain-hawk,
And heard at dawn the unrivall'd one, the hermit thrush
    from the swamp-cedars,
Solitary, singing in the West, I strike up for a New World.

The poet deliberately studied the habits of
such creatures as the fishing hawk.

Boyhood's times, the clam-digging, bare-foot, and
fishing excursions, or of later years,
the little voyages down and out New York bay . . .

*Brooklyn, Long Island, was a busy port according
to this 1847 drawing by Edwin Whitefield.*

As I write, the whole experience comes back to me after
the lapse of forty and more years — the soothing rustle of the
waves, and the saline smell — boyhood's times, the clam-
digging, bare-foot, and with trowsers roll'd up — hauling down
the creek — the perfume of the sedge-meadows — the hay-boat,
and the chowder and fishing excursions; — or, of later years,
little voyages down and out New York bay, in the pilot
boats. Those same later years, also, while living in Brooklyn,
(1836-'50) I went regularly every week in the mild seasons
down to Coney Island, at that time a long, bare unfrequented
shore, which I had all to myself, and where I loved, after
bathing, to race up and down the hard sand, and declaim
Homer or Shakspere to the surf and sea gulls by the hour.
But I am getting ahead too rapidly, and must keep more in
my traces.

From PAUMANOK, AND MY LIFE ON IT
AS CHILD AND YOUNG MAN

Afoot and light-hearted I take to the open road,
Healthy, free, the world before me,
The long brown path before me leading wherever I choose.
. . . Strong and content I travel the open road.

II

The Outsetting Bard

"*I am the poet of the woman the same as the man.*"

Algimantas Kezys

From SONG OF MYSELF

I am the poet of the Body and I am the poet of the Soul,
The pleasures of heaven are with me and the pains of hell
    are with me,
The first I graft and increase upon myself, the latter I
    translate into a new tongue.

I am the poet of the woman the same as the man,
And I say it is as great to be a woman as to be a man,
And I say there is nothing greater than the mother of men.
I chant the chant of dilation and pride,
We have had ducking and deprecating about enough,
I show that size is only development.

The pleasures of heaven are with me . . .

Have you outstript the rest? are you the President?
It is a trifle, they will more than arrive there every one, and
   still pass on.

I am he that walks with the tender and growing night,
I call to the earth and sea half-held by the night.

Press close bare-bosom'd night — press close magnetic
   nourishing night!
Night of south winds — night of the large few stars!
Still nodding night — mad naked summer night.

Smile O voluptuous cool-breath'd earth!
Earth of the slumbering and liquid trees!
Earth of departed sunset — earth of the mountains misty-topt!
Earth of the vitreous pour of the full moon just tinged with
   blue!
Earth of shine and dark mottling the tide of the river!
Earth of the limpid gray of clouds brighter and clearer for
   my sake!
Far-swooping elbow'd earth — rich apple-blossom'd earth!
Smile, for your lover comes.

Sit a while dear son,
Here are biscuits to eat and here is milk to drink,
But as soon as you sleep and renew yourself in sweet clothes,
   I kiss you with a good-by kiss and open the gate for your
   egress hence.

Long enough have you dream'd contemptible dreams,
Now I wash the gum from your eyes,
You must habit yourself to the dazzle of the light and of
   every moment of your life.

Long have you timidly waded holding a plank by the shore,
Now I will you to be a bold swimmer,
To jump off in the midst of the sea, rise again, nod to me,
   shout, and laughingly dash with your hair.

Whitman wrote, "I say there is nothing
greater than the mother of men."

The earth expanding right hand and left hand . . .

From SONG OF THE OPEN ROAD

Afoot and light-hearted I take to the open road,
Healthy, free, the world before me,
The long brown path before me leading wherever I choose.

Henceforth I ask not good-fortune, I myself am good-fortune,
Henceforth I whimper no more, postpone no more, need
    nothing,
Done with indoor complaints, libraries, querulous criticisms,
Strong and content I travel the open road.

The earth, that is sufficient,
I do not want the constellations any nearer,
I know they are very well where they are,
I know they suffice for those who belong to them.

The earth expanding right hand and left hand,
The picture alive, every part in its best light,
The music falling in where it is wanted, and stopping where
    it is not wanted,
The cheerful voice of the public road, the gay fresh sentiment
    of the road.

O highway I travel, do you say to me *Do not leave me?*
Do you say *Venture not—if you leave me you are lost?*
Do you say *I am already prepared, I am well-beaten and
    undenied, adhere to me?*

O public road, I say back I am not afraid to leave you, yet I
    love you,
You express me better than I can express myself,
You shall be more to me than my poem.

I think heroic deeds were all conceiv'd in the open air, and
    all free poems also,
I think I could stop here myself and do miracles,
I think whatever I shall meet on the road I shall like, and
    whoever beholds me shall like me,
I think whoever I see must be happy.

*Opposite: Whitman was convinced that heroic deeds
and free poems were all conceived in the open air.*

*A scene in the San Juan Mountains
in southwestern Colorado.*

I, now thirty-seven years old in perfect health begin,
Hoping to cease not till death . . .

From SONG OF MYSELF

I celebrate myself, and sing myself,
And what I assume you shall assume,
For every atom belonging to me as good belongs to you.

I loafe and invite my soul,
I lean and loafe at my ease observing a spear of summer
    grass.
My tongue, every atom of my blood, form'd from this soil,
    this air,
Born here of parents born here from parents the same, and
    their parents the same,
I, now thirty-seven years old in perfect health begin,
Hoping to cease not till death.

Creeds and schools in abeyance,
Retiring back a while sufficed at what they are, but never
    forgotten,
I harbor for good or bad, I permit to speak at every hazard,
Nature without check with original energy.

From STARTING FROM PAUMANOK

The soul,
Forever and forever — longer than soil is brown and solid —
    longer than water ebbs and flows.

I will make the poems of materials, for I think they are to
    be the most spiritual poems,
And I will make the poems of my body and of mortality,
For I think I shall then supply myself with the poems of my
    soul and of immortality.

I will not make poems with reference to parts,
But I will make poems, songs, thoughts, with reference to
    ensemble,
And I will not sing with reference to a day, but with
    reference to all days,
And I will not make a poem nor the least part of a poem but
    has reference to the soul,
Because having look'd at the objects of the universe, I find
    there is no one nor any particle of one but has reference
    to the soul.

From SONG OF MYSELF

This day before dawn I ascended a hill and look'd at the
    crowded heaven,
And I said to my spirit *When we become the enfolders of
those orbs, and the pleasure and knowledge of every thing
in them, shall we be fill'd and satisfied then?*
And my spirit said *No, we but level that lift to pass and
continue beyond.*

You are also asking me questions and I hear you,
I answer that I cannot answer, you must find out for yourself.

From A SONG OF JOYS

O the joy of my spirit—it is uncaged—it darts like lightning!
It is not enough to have this globe or a certain time,
I will have thousands of globes and all time.

From SONG OF MYSELF

There is that in me—I do not know what it is—but I know it
    is in me.

Wrench'd and sweaty—calm and cool then my body becomes,
I sleep—I sleep long.

I do not know it—it is without name—it is a word unsaid,
It is not in any dictionary, utterance, symbol.

Something it swings on more than the earth I swing on,
To it the creation is the friend whose embracing awakes me.

Perhaps I might tell more. Outlines! I plead for my brothers
    and sisters.

Do you see O my brothers and sisters?
It is not chaos or death—it is form, union, plan—it is eternal
    life—it is Happiness.

Gene Ahrens

*The Barnegat Lighthouse on the
New Jersey shore.*

Gene Ahrens

The plenteousness of space was a joy to Whitman.

Let the preacher preach in his pulpit, let the lawyer plead,
I give you myself before preaching or law . . .

From A SONG OF JOYS

O to realize space!
The plenteousness of all, that there are no bounds,
To emerge and be of the sky, of the sun and moon and flying
    clouds, as one with them.

O the joy of a manly self-hood!
To be servile to none, to defer to none, not to any tyrant
    known or unknown,
To walk with erect carriage, a step springy and elastic,
To look with calm gaze or with a flashing eye,
To speak with a full and sonorous voice out of a broad chest,
To confront with your personality all the other personalities
    of the earth.

From SONG OF THE OPEN ROAD

Allons! the road is before us!
It is safe — I have tried it — my own feet have tried it well —
    be not detain'd!
Let the paper remain on the desk unwritten, and the book on
    the shelf unopen'd!

Let the tools remain in the workshop! let the money remain
    unearn'd!
Let the school stand! mind not the cry of the teacher!
Let the preacher preach in his pulpit! let the lawyer plead
    in the court, and the judge expound the law.

Camerado, I give you my hand!
I give you my love more precious than money,
I give you myself before preaching or law;
Will you give me yourself? Will you come travel with me?
Shall we stick by each other as long as we live?

Gene Ahrens

Sugar Hill, a church in New Hampshire.

Here is not merely a nation but a teeming nation of nations. Here the performance spreads with crampless and flowing breadth and showers its prolific and splendid extravagance. One sees it must indeed own the riches of the summer and winter . . .

III

America "With Crampless and Flowing Breadth"

The United States are the greatest poem . . .

Artstreet

*Fishermen will soon gather
their nets and set out.*

The Americans of all nations at any time upon the earth have probably the fullest poetical nature. The United States themselves are essentially the greatest poem. In the history of the earth hitherto the largest and most stirring appear tame and orderly to their ampler largeness and stir. Here at last is something in the doings of man that corresponds with the broadcast doings of the day and night. Here is not merely a nation but a teeming nation of nations. Here is action untied from strings necessarily blind to particulars and details magnificently moving in vast masses. Here is the hospitality which forever indicates heroes. . . . Here are the roughs and beards and space and ruggedness and nonchalance that the soul loves. Here the performance disdaining the trivial unapproached in the tremendous audacity of its crowds and groupings and the push of its perspective spreads with crampless and flowing breadth and showers its prolific and splendid extravagance. One sees it must indeed own the riches of the summer and winter, and need never be bankrupt while corn grows from the ground or the orchards drop apples or the bays contain fish or men beget children upon women. . . .

From PREFACE TO THE FIRST EDITION OF
LEAVES OF GRASS

I HEAR AMERICA SINGING

I hear America singing, the varied carols I hear,
Those of mechanics, each one singing his as it should be
    blithe and strong,
The carpenter singing his as he measures his plank or beam,
The mason singing his as he makes ready for work, or leaves
    off work,
The boatman singing what belongs to him in his boat, the
    deckhand singing on the steamboat deck,
The shoemaker singing as he sits on his bench, the hatter
    singing as he stands,
The wood-cutter's song, the ploughboy's on his way in the
    morning, or at noon intermission or at sundown,
The delicious singing of the mother, or of the young wife at
    work, or of the girl sewing or washing,
Each singing what belongs to him or her and to none else,
The day what belongs to the day—at night the party of
    young fellows, robust, friendly,
Singing with open mouths their strong melodious songs.

While corn grows from the ground, said Whitman, America need never be bankrupt.

Gene Ahrens

Seeking what is yet unfound, Whitman looked westward.

FACING WEST
FROM CALIFORNIA'S SHORES

Facing west from California's shores,
Inquiring, tireless, seeking what is yet unfound,
I, a child, very old, over waves, towards the house of
    maternity, the land of migrations, look afar,
Look off the shores of my Western sea, the circle almost
    circled;
For starting westward from Hindustan, from the vales of
    Kashmere,
From Asia, from the north, from the God, the sage, and the
    hero,
From the south, from the flowery peninsulas and the spice
    islands,
Long having wander'd since, round the earth having
    wander'd.
Now I face home again, very pleas'd and joyous,
(But where is what I started for so long ago?
And why is it yet unfound?)

I will make divine magnetic lands . . .

ON JOURNEYS THROUGH THE STATES

On journeys through the States we start,
(Ay through the world, urged by these songs,
Sailing henceforth to every land, to every sea,)
We willing learners of all, teachers of all, and lovers of all.

We have watch'd the seasons dispensing themselves and
    passing on,
And have said, Why should not a man or woman do as much
    as the seasons, and effuse as much?

We dwell a while in every city and town,
We pass through Kanada, the North-east, the vast valley of
    the Mississippi, and the Southern States,
We confer on equal terms with each of the States,
We make trial of ourselves and invite men and women to
    hear,
We say to ourselves, Remember, fear not, be candid,
    promulge the body and the soul,
Dwell a while and pass on, be copious, temperate, chaste,
    magnetic,
And what you effuse may then return as the seasons return,
And may be just as much as the seasons.

FOR YOU O DEMOCRACY

Come, I will make the continent indissoluble,
I will make the most splendid race the sun ever shone upon,
I will make divine magnetic lands,
        With the love of comrades,
            With the life-long love of comrades.

I will plant companionship thick as trees along all the rivers
        of America, and along the shores of the great lakes, and
        all over the prairies,
I will make inseparable cities with their arms about each
        other's necks,
        By the love of comrades,
            By the manly love of comrades.

For you these from me, O Democracy, to serve you ma
        femme!
For you, for you I am trilling these songs.

With all thy wide geographies, manifold, different, distant,
One common indivisible destiny for All . . .

From SONG OF THE EXPOSITION

Gene Ahrens

And thou America,
Thy offspring towering e'er so high, yet higher Thee above
    all towering,
With Victory on thy left, and at thy right hand Law;
Thou Union holding all, fusing, absorbing, tolerating all,
Thee, ever thee, I sing.

Thou, also thou, a World,
With all thy wide geographies, manifold, different, distant,
Rounded by thee in one — one common orbic language,
One common indivisible destiny for All.

And by the spells which ye vouchsafe to those your ministers
    in earnest,
I here personify and call my themes, to make them pass
    before ye.

Behold, America! (and thou, ineffable guest and sister!)
For thee come trooping up thy waters and thy lands;
Behold! thy fields and farms, thy far-off woods and mountains,
As in procession coming.

Behold, the sea itself,
And on its limitless, heaving breast, the ships;
See, where their white sails, bellying in the wind, speckle the
    green and blue,
See, the steamers coming and going, steaming in or out of
    port,
See, dusky and undulating, the long pennants of smoke.

Behold, in Oregon, far in the north and west,
Or in Maine, far in the north and east, thy cheerful axemen,
Wielding all day their axes.
Behold, on the lakes, thy pilots at their wheels, thy oarsmen,
How the ash writhes under those muscular arms!

There by the furnace, and there by the anvil,
Behold thy sturdy blacksmiths swinging their sledges,
Overhand so steady, overhand they turn and fall with joyous
    clank,
Like a tumult of laughter.

Nature formed America
long before her people did.

Mark the spirit of invention everywhere, thy rapid patents,
Thy continual workshops, foundries, risen or rising,
See, from their chimneys how the tall flame-fires stream.

Mark, thy interminable farms, North, South,
Thy wealthy daughter-states, Eastern and Western,
The varied products of Ohio, Pennsylvania, Missouri, Georgia,
    Texas, and the rest,
Thy limitless crops, grass, wheat, sugar, oil, corn, rice, hemp,
    hops,
Thy barns all fill'd, the endless freight-train and the bulging
    storehouse,
The grapes that ripen on thy vines, the apples in thy orchards,
Thy incalculable lumber, beef, pork, potatoes, thy coal, thy
    gold and silver,
The inexhaustible iron in thy mines.

All thine, O sacred Union!
Ships, farms, shops, barns, factories, mines,
City and State, North, South, item and aggregate,
We dedicate, dread Mother, all to thee!

Protectress absolute, thou! bulwark of all!
For well we know that while thou givest each and all,
    (generous as God,)
Without thee neither all nor each, nor land, home,
Nor ship, nor mine, nor any here this day secure,
Nor aught, nor any day secure.

Whitman foresaw vast factories replacing the shops of his time.

All thine, O sacred Union! Ships, farms, shops, barns, factories . . .

From I SING THE BODY ELECTRIC

I knew a man, a common farmer, the father of five sons,
And in them the fathers of sons, and in them the fathers of
    sons.

This man was of wonderful vigor, calmness, beauty of person,
The shape of his head, the pale yellow and white of his hair
        and beard, the immeasurable meaning of his black eyes,
        the richness and breadth of his manners,
These I used to go and visit him to see, he was wise also,
He was six feet tall, he was over eighty years old, his sons
        were massive, clean, bearded, tan-faced, handsome,
They and his daughters loved him, all who saw him loved
    him,
They did not love him by allowance, they loved him with
    personal love,
He drank water only, the blood show'd like scarlet through
    the clear-brown skin of his face,
He was a frequent gunner and fisher, he sail'd his boat
    himself, he had a fine one presented to him by a
    ship-joiner, he had fowling-pieces presented to him by
    men that loved him,
When he went with his five sons and many grand-sons to
    hunt or fish, you would pick him out as the most
    beautiful and vigorous of the gang,
You would wish long and long to be with him, you would
    wish to sit by him in the boat that you and he might
    touch each other.

From SONG OF MYSELF

The negro holds firmly the reins of his four horses, the block
    swags underneath on its tied-over chain,
The negro that drives the long dray of the stone-yard,
    steady and tall he stands pois'd on one leg on the
    string-piece,
His blue shirt exposes his ample neck and breast and loosens
    over his hip-band,
His glance is calm and commanding, he tosses the slouch of
    his hat away from his forehead,
The sun falls on his crispy hair and mustache, falls on the
    black of his polish'd and perfect limbs.

I behold the picturesque giant and love him, and I do not
    stop there,
I go with the team also.

Today thou groan'st with riches, thou laughest loud
with ache of great possessions . . .

Artstreet

I realize . . . that not Nature alone is great in her fields
of freedom and the open air, in her storms, the shows
of night and day, the mountains, forests, sea — but in the
artificial, the work of man too is equally great — in
this profusion of teeming humanity — in these ingenuities,
streets, goods, houses, ships — these hurrying, feverish,
electric crowds of men, their complicated business
genius (not least among the geniuses), and all this mighty,
many-threaded wealth and industry concentrated here . . . .

From DEMOCRATIC VISTAS

From THE RETURN OF THE HEROES

Fecund America — to-day,
Thou art all over set in births and joys!
Thou groan'st with riches, thy wealth clothes thee as a
    swathing-garment,
Thou laughest loud with ache of great possessions,
A myriad-twining life like interlacing vines binds all thy vast
    demesne,
As some huge ship freighted to water's edge thou ridest into
    port,
As rain falls from the heaven and vapors rise from earth, so
    have the precious values fallen upon thee and risen out
    of thee;
Thou envy of the globe! thou miracle!
Thou, bathed, choked, swimming in plenty,
Thou lucky Mistress of the tranquil barns,
Thou Prairie Dame that sittest in the middle and lookest out
    upon thy world, and lookest East and lookest West,
Dispensatress, that by a word givest a thousand miles, a
    million farms, and missest nothing,
Thou all-acceptress — thou hospitable, (thou only art
    hospitable as God is hospitable.)

The poet saw America's wealth and industry
as "mighty" and "many-threaded."

A New Jersey farm like hundreds Whitman saw and celebrated.

Gene Ahrens

From SONG OF THE EXPOSITION

Now here and these and hence in peace, all thine O Flag!
And here and hence for thee, O universal Muse! and thou
    for them!
And here and hence O Union, all the work and workmen
    thine!
None separate from thee—henceforth One only, we and
    thou,
(For the blood of the children, what is it, only the blood
    maternal?
And lives and works, what are they all at last, except the
    roads to faith and death?)

While we rehearse our measureless wealth, it is for thee,
    dear Mother,
We own it all and several to-day indissoluble in thee;
Think not our chant, our show, merely for products gross
    and lucre—it is for thee, the soul in thee, electric,
    spiritual!
Our farms, inventions, crops, we own in thee! cities and
    States in thee!
Our freedom all in thee! our very lives in thee!

Beat! beat! drums! — blow! bugles! blow!
Through the windows — through doors — burst like a ruthless
    force,
Into the solemn church, and scatter the congregation,
Into the school where the scholar is studying . . .

IV
The Beat of the Drum

I hear the tramp of armies, I hear the challenging sentry,
I hear the shouts of millions of men, I hear Liberty! . . .

Artstreet

With the thunder and lightning of drums and bugles, the Civil War burst upon the United States like a ruthless storm.

BEAT! BEAT! DRUMS!

Beat! beat! drums!—blow! bugles! blow!
Through the windows—through doors—burst like a ruthless
    force,
Into the solemn church, and scatter the congregation,
Into the school where the scholar is studying;
Leave not the bridegroom quiet—no happiness must he
    have now with his bride,
Nor the peaceful farmer any peace, ploughing his field or
    gathering his grain,
So fierce you whirr and pound you drums—so shrill you
    bugles blow.

From SONG OF THE BANNER AT DAYBREAK

I hear and see not strips of cloth alone,
I hear the tramp of armies, I hear the challenging sentry,
I hear the jubilant shouts of millions of men, I hear Liberty!
I hear the drums beat and the trumpets blowing,
I myself move abroad swift-rising flying then,
I use the wings of the land-bird and use the wings of the
    sea-bird, and look down as from a height,
I do not deny the precious results of peace, I see populous
    cities with wealth incalculable,
I see numberless farms, I see the farmers working in their
    fields or barns,
I see mechanics working, I see buildings everywhere founded,
    going up, or finish'd,
I see trains of cars swiftly speeding along railroad tracks
    drawn by the locomotives,
I see the stores, depots, of Boston, Baltimore, Charleston,
    New Orleans,
I see far in the West the immense area of grain, I dwell
    awhile hovering,
I pass to the lumber forests of the North, and again to the
    Southern plantation, and again to California;
Sweeping the whole I see the countless profit, the busy
    gatherings, earn'd wages,
See the Identity formed out of thirty-eight spacious and
    haughty States, (and many more to come,)
See forts on the shores of harbors, see ships sailing in and
    out;
Then over all, (aye! aye!) my little and lengthen'd pennant
    shaped like a sword,
Runs swiftly up indicating war and defiance—and now the
    halyards have rais'd it,
Side of my banner broad and blue, side of my starry banner,
Discarding peace over all the sea and land.

*The luxuriant countryside would soon
be ravaged by fire and cannon.*

It was a curious sight to see those shadowy columns
moving through the night. I stood unobserv'd in the darkness
and watch'd them long. The mud was very deep. The men
had their usual burdens, overcoats, knapsacks, guns
and blankets. Along and along they filed by me, with often
a laugh, a song, a cheerful word, but never once a murmur.
It may have been odd, but I never before so realized
the majesty and reality of the American people *en masse*.
It fell upon me like a great awe . . . .

From SPECIMEN DAYS

AS TOILSOME I WANDER'D VIRGINIA'S WOODS

As toilsome I wander'd Virginia's woods,
To the music of rustling leaves kick'd by my feet,
    (For 'twas autumn,)
I mark'd at the foot of a tree the grave of a soldier,
Mortally wounded he and buried on the retreat,
    (easily all could I understand,)
The halt of a mid-day hour, when up! no time to lose—yet
    this sign left,
On a tablet scrawl'd and nail'd on the tree by the grave,
Bold, cautious, true, and my loving comrade.

Long, long I muse, then on my way go wandering;
Many a changeful season to follow, and many a scene of life,
Yet at times through changeful season and scene, abrupt,
    alone, or in the crowded street,
Comes before me the unknown soldier's grave, comes the
    inscription rude in Virginia's woods,
Bold, cautious, true, and my loving comrade.

"Boy in the road at Fredericksburg," a photograph by Mathew Brady.

I resign'd myself to sit by the wounded and soothe them . . .

"Wounded soldier given a drink from a canteen," a sketch by Winslow Homer.

From THE WOUND-DRESSER

An old man bending I come among new faces,
Years looking backward resuming in answer to children,
Come tell us old man, as from young men and maidens
    that love me,
(Arous'd and angry, I'd thought to beat the alarum, and
    urge relentless war,
But soon my fingers fail'd me, my face droop'd and I resign'd
    myself,
To sit by the wounded and soothe them, or silently watch
    the dead;)
Years hence of these scenes, of these furious passions, these
    chances,
Of unsurpass'd heroes, (was one side so brave? the other
    was equally brave;)
Now be witness again, paint the mightiest armies of earth,
Of those armies so rapid so wondrous what saw you to tell
    us?
What stays with you latest and deepest? of curious panics,
Of hard-fought engagements or sieges tremendous what
    deepest remains?

A SIGHT IN CAMP IN THE DAYBREAK GRAY AND DIM

A sight in camp in the daybreak gray and dim,
As from my tent I emerge so early sleepless,
As slow I walk in the cool fresh air the path near by the
    hospital tent,
Three forms I see on stretchers lying, brought out there
    untended lying,
Over each the blanket spread, ample brownish woolen
    blanket,
Gray and heavy blanket, folding, covering all.

Curious I halt and silent stand,
Then with light fingers I from the face of the nearest the
    first just lift the blanket;
Who are you elderly man so gaunt and grim, with well-gray'd
    hair, and flesh all sunken about the eyes?
Who are you my dear comrade?

Then to the second I step — and who are you my child and
    darling?
Who are you sweet boy with cheeks yet blooming?

Then to the third — a face nor child nor old, very calm, as of
    beautiful yellow-white ivory;
Young man I think I know you — I think this face is the face
    of the Christ himself,
Dead and divine and brother of all, and here again he lies.

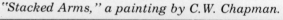

"Stacked Arms," a painting by C.W. Chapman.

Who are you sweet boy with cheeks yet blooming? . . .

"*Young Union Warrior,*" *a painting by Winslow Homer*

Down in the fields all prospers well, but now from the fields come father, here's a letter from our Pete . . .

The father works and waits alone.

COME UP FROM THE FIELDS FATHER

Come up from the fields father, here's a letter from our Pete,
And come to the front door mother, here's a letter from thy
    dear son.

Lo, 'tis autumn,
Lo, where the trees, deeper green, yellower and redder,
Cool and sweeten Ohio's villages with leaves fluttering in the
    moderate wind,
Where apples ripe in the orchards hang and grapes on the
    trellis'd vines,
(Smell you the smell of the grapes on the vines?
Smell you the buckwheat where the bees were lately
    buzzing?)

Above all, lo, the sky so calm, so transparent after the rain,
    and with wondrous clouds,
Below too, all calm, all vital and beautiful, and the farm
    prospers well.

Down in the fields all prospers well,
But now from the fields come father, come at the daughter's
    call,
And come to the entry mother, to the front door come right
    away.

Fast as she can she hurries, something ominous, her steps
    trembling,
She does not tarry to smooth her hair nor adjust her cap.

Open the envelope quickly,
O this is not our son's writing, yet his name is sign'd,

O a strange hand writes for our dear son, O stricken
    mother's soul!
All swims before her eyes, flashes with black, she catches the
    main words only,
Sentences broken, *gunshot wound in the breast, cavalry
skirmish, taken to hospital,*
At present low, but will soon be better.

Ah now the single figure to me,
Amid all teeming and wealthy Ohio with all its cities and
    farms,
Sickly white in the face and dull in the head, very faint,
By the jamb of a door leans.

60

Grieve not so, dear mother, (the just-grown daughter speaks
   through her sobs,
The little sisters huddle around speechless and dismay'd,)
See, dearest mother, the letter says Pete will soon be better.

Alas poor boy, he will never be better, (nor may-be needs to
   be better, that brave and simple soul,)
While they stand at home at the door he is dead already,
The only son is dead.

But the mother needs to be better,
She with thin form presently drest in black,
By day her meals untouch'd, then at night fitfully sleeping,
   often waking,
In the midnight waking, weeping, longing with one deep
   longing,
O that she might withdraw unnoticed, silent from life escape
   and withdraw,
To follow, to seek, to be with her dear dead son.

From WHEN LILACS
LAST IN THE DOORYARD BLOOM'D

When lilacs last in the dooryard bloom'd,
And the great star early droop'd in the western sky in the
   night,
I mourn'd, and yet shall mourn with ever-returning spring.

Ever-returning spring, trinity sure to me you bring,
Lilac blooming perennial and drooping star in the west,
And thought of him I love.

O powerful western fallen star!
O shades of night — O moody, tearful night!
O great star disappear'd — O the black murk that hides
   the star!
O cruel hands that hold me powerless — O helpless soul
   of me!
O harsh surrounding cloud that will not free my soul.

I saw battle-corpses, myriads of them,
And the white skeletons of young men — I saw them;
I saw the debris and debris of all the dead soldiers of
   the war;
But I saw they were not as was thought;
They themselves were fully at rest — they suffer'd not;
The living remain'd and suffer'd — the mother suffer'd,
And the wife and the child, and the musing comrade
   suffer'd,
And the armies that remain'd suffer'd.

Away with themes of war! away with war itself! That hell unpent . . .

Historic Burnside Bridge, the site of the Battle of Antietam.

From SONG OF THE EXPOSITION

Away with themes of war! away with war itself!
Hence from my shuddering sight to never more return that
      show of blacken'd, mutilated corpses!
That hell unpent and raid of blood, fit for wild tigers or for
      lop-tongued wolves, not reasoning men,
And in its stead speed industry's campaigns,
With thy undaunted armies, engineering,
Thy pennants labor, loosen'd to the breeze,
Thy bugles sounding loud and clear.

VIGIL STRANGE I KEPT
ON THE FIELD ONE NIGHT

Vigil strange I kept on the field one night;
When you my son and my comrade dropt at my side that
    day,
One look I but gave which your dear eyes return'd with a
    look I shall never forget,
One touch of your hand to mine O boy, reach'd up as you
    lay on the ground,
Then onward I sped in the battle, the even-contested battle,
Till late in the night reliev'd to the place at last again I
    made my way,
Found you in death so cold dear comrade, found your body
    son of responding kisses, (never again on earth
    responding,)
Bared your face in the starlight, curious the scene, cool
    blew the moderate night-wind,
Long there and then in vigil I stood, dimly around me the
    battlefield spreading,
Vigil wondrous and vigil sweet there in the fragrant silent
    night,
But not a tear fell, not even a long-drawn sigh, long, long
    I gazed,
Then on the earth partially reclining sat by your side leaning
    my chin in my hands,
Passing sweet hours, immortal and mystic hours with you
    dearest comrade—not a tear, not a word,
Vigil of silence, love and death, vigil for you my son and my
    soldier,
As onward silently stars aloft, eastward new ones upward
    stole,
Vigil final for you brave boy, (I could not save you, swift
    was your death,
I faithfully loved you and cared for you living, I think we
    shall surely meet again.)

Till at latest lingering of the night, indeed just as the dawn
    appear'd,
My comrade I wrapt in his blanket, envelop'd over head
    and carefully under feet,
And there and then and bathed by the rising sun, my son
    in his grave, in his rude-dug grave I deposited,
Ending my vigil strange with that, vigil of night and
    battle-field dim,
Vigil for boy of responding kisses, (never again on earth
    responding,)
Vigil for comrade swiftly slain, vigil I never forget, how as
    day brighten'd,
I rose from the chill ground and folded my soldier well in
    his blanket,
And buried him where he fell.

All expected from heaven or from the highest,[the poet] is rapport with: in the sight of daybreak or a scene of the winter woods or the presence of children playing. . . . His love above all love has leisure and expanse . . .

V
In the Sight of Daybreak

The known universe has one complete lover and that is
the greatest poet. He consumes an eternal passion
and is indifferent which chance happens and which possible
contingency of fortune or misfortune and persuades
daily and hourly his delicious pay. What balks or breaks
others is fuel for his burning progress to contact and
amorous joy. Other proportions of the reception of pleasure
dwindle to nothing to his proportions. All expected from
heaven or from the highest he is rapport with in the
sight of the daybreak or a scene of the winter woods or the
presence of children playing or with his arm round the
neck of a man or woman. His love above all love has leisure
and expanse . . . . he leaves room ahead of himself.
He is no irresolute or suspicious lover . . . he is sure . . .
he scorns intervals. His experience and the showers
and thrills are not for nothing. Nothing can jar him . . .
suffering and darkness cannot—death and fear cannot. To
him complaint and jealousy and envy are corpses buried
and rotten in the earth . . . he saw them buried. The
sea is not surer of the shore or the shore of the sea than he
is the fruition of his love and of all perfection and beauty . . .

From PREFACE TO THE FIRST EDITION OF
LEAVES OF GRASS

Dilapidated, fenceless, and trodden with war as Virginia
is, wherever I move across her surface, I find myself
rous'd to surprise and admiration. What capacity for products,
improvements, human life, nourishment and expansion.
Everywhere that I have been in the old Dominion, (the subtle
mockery of that title now!) such thoughts have fill'd me.
The soil is yet far above the average of any of the northern
States. And how full of breadth the scenery, everywhere
distant mountains, everywhere convenient rivers. Even yet
prodigal in forest woods, and surely eligible for all the
fruits, orchards, and flowers. The skies and atmosphere
most luscious, as I feel certain, from more than a year's
residence in the State, and movements hither and yon.
I should say very healthy, as a general thing. Then a rich
and elastic quality, by night and by day. The sun rejoices in
his strength, dazzling and burning, and yet, to me, never
unpleasantly weakening. It is not the panting tropical heat,
but invigorates. The north tempers it. The nights are often
unsurpassable. Last evening (Feb. 8,) I saw the first of
the new moon, the outlined old moon clear along with it; the
sky and air so clear, such transparent hues of color, it
seem'd to me I had never really seen the new moon before.
It was the thinnest cut crescent possible. It hung delicate
just above the sulky shadow of the Blue mountains. Ah,
if it might prove an omen and good prophecy for this
unhappy State.

From SPECIMEN DAYS (Virginia)

The known universe has one complete lover . . .

...a's Shenandoah Valley (above) and Blue Ridge Mountains (below).
...th-century America was ripe for a poet of Whitman's stature
...understand and communicate her sprawling, picturesque land.

*On the beach at night alone, I think a thought of the clef
of the universes and of the future . . . .*

From SONG OF THE BANNER
AT DAYBREAK

Fresh and rosy red the sun is mounting high,
On floats the sea in distant blue careering through its
    channels,
On floats the wind over the breast of the sea setting in
    toward land,
The steady wind from west or west-by-south,
Floating so buoyant with milk-white foam on the waters.

But I am not the sea nor the red sun,
I am not the wind with girlish laughter,
Not the immense wind which strengthens, not the wind which
    lashes,
Not the spirit that ever lashes its own body to terror and
    death,
But I am that which unseen comes and sings, sings, sings,
Which babbles in brooks and scoots in showers on the land,
Which birds know in the woods mornings and evenings,
And the shore-sands know and the hissing wave, and that
    banner and pennant,
Aloft there flapping and flapping.

ON THE BEACH AT NIGHT ALONE

On the beach at night alone,
As the old mother sways her to and fro singing her husky
    song,
As I watch the bright stars shining, I think a thought of the
    clef of the universes and of the future.
A vast similitude interlocks all,
All spheres, grown, ungrown, small, large, suns, moons,
    planets,
All distances of place however wide,
All distances of time, all inanimate forms,
All souls, all living bodies though they be ever so different, or
    in different worlds,
All gaseous, watery, vegetable, mineral processes, the fishes,
    the brutes,
All nations, colors, barbarisms, civilizations, languages,
All identities that have existed or may exist on this globe,
    or any globe,
All lives and deaths, all of the past, present, future,
This vast similitude spans them, and always has spann'd,
And shall forever span them and compactly hold and enclose
    them.

*The late sun hovering over a vast expanse of water
evokes the timelessness within the universe.*

The known universe has one complete lover . . .

Photos by Gene Ahrens

Virginia's Shenandoah Valley (above) and Blue Ridge Mountains (below).
Nineteenth-century America was ripe for a poet of Whitman's stature
who could understand and communicate her sprawling, picturesque land.

How strong, vital, enduring! how dumbly eloquent!
What suggestions of imperturbability and *being,* as against
the human trait of mere *seeming.* Then the qualities,
almost emotional, palpably artistic, heroic, of a tree; so
innocent and harmless, yet so savage. It *is,* yet says nothing.
How it rebukes by its tough and equable serenity all
weathers, this gusty-temper'd little whiffet, man, that runs
indoors at a mite of rain or snow. . . .

From SPECIMEN DAYS (The Lesson of a Tree)

I SAW IN LOUISIANA A LIVE-OAK GROWING

I saw in Louisiana a live-oak growing,
All alone stood it and the moss hung down from the
    branches,
Without any companion it grew there uttering joyous leaves
    of dark green,
And its look, rude, unbending, lusty, made me think of
    myself,
But I wonder'd how it could utter joyous leaves standing
    alone there without its friend near, for I knew I could not,
And I broke off a twig with a certain number of leaves upon
    it, and twined around it a little moss,
And brought it away, and I have placed it in sight, in my
    room,
It is not needed to remind me as of my own dear friends,
(For I believe lately I think of little else than of them,)
Yet it remains to me a curious token, it makes me think of
    manly love;
For all that, and though the live-oak glistens there in
    Louisiana solitary in a wide flat space, ·
Uttering joyous leaves all its life without a friend a lover
    near,
I know very well I could not.

A promise of blossoms bursting forth in the fresh, free, open air.

NOT MEAGRE, LATENT BOUGHS ALONE

Not meagre, latent boughs alone, O songs! (scaly and bare,
    like eagles' talons,)
But haply for some sunny day (who knows?) some future
    spring, some summer — bursting forth,
To verdant leaves, or sheltering shade — to nourishing fruit,
Apples and grapes — the stalwart limbs of trees emerging —
    the fresh, free, open air,
And love and faith, like scented roses blooming.

But haply for some sunny day, the promise of some future spring fulfilled . . .

From SONG OF MYSELF

I think I could turn and live with animals, they're so placid
    and self-contain'd,
I stand and look at them long and long.

They do not sweat and whine about their condition,
They do not lie awake in the dark and weep for their sins,
They do not make me sick discussing their duty to God,
Not one is dissatisfied, not one is demented with the mania
    of owning things,
Not one kneels to another, nor to his kind that lived
    thousands of years ago,
Not one is respectable or unhappy over the whole earth.

The seeming contentment of this muskrat would have provoked Whitman's envy.

*Each day, each hour of the day, is a miracle of light and color —
enough to make a colorist delirious . . .*

THE OX-TAMER

In a far-away northern county in the placid pastoral region,
Lives my farmer friend, the theme of my recitative, a famous
    tamer of oxen,
There they bring him the three-year-olds and the four-year-
    olds to break them,
He will take the wildest steer in the world and break him
    and tame him,
He will go fearless without any whip where the young bullock
    chafes up and down the yard,
The bullock's head tosses restless high in the air with raging
    eyes,
Yet see you! how soon his rage subsides—how soon this
    tamer tames him;
See you! on the farms hereabouts a hundred oxen young and
    old, and he is the man who has tamed them,
They all know him, all are affectionate to him;
See you! some are such beautiful animals, so lofty looking;
Some are buff-color'd, some mottled, one has a white line
    running along his back, some are brindled,
Some have wide flaring horns (a good sign)—see you! the
    bright hides,
See, the two with stars on their foreheads—see, the round
    bodies and broad backs,
How straight and square they stand on their legs—what
    fine sagacious eyes!
How they watch their tamer—they wish him near them—
    how they turn to look after him!
What yearning expression! how uneasy they are when he
    moves away from them;
Now I marvel what it can be he appears to them, (books,
    politics, poems, depart—all else departs,)
I confess I envy only his fascination—my silent, illiterate
    friend,
Whom a hundred oxen love there in his life on farms,
In the northern country far, in the placid pastoral region.

Down every day in the solitude of the creek. A serene
autumn sun and westerly breeze today as I sit here,
the water surface prettily moving in wind-ripples before me.
On a stout old beech at the edge, decayed and slanting,
almost fallen to the stream, yet with life and leaves in its
mossy limbs, a gray squirrel, exploring, runs up and
down, flirts his tail, leaps to the ground, sits on his haunches
upright as he sees me, (a Darwinian hint?) and then
races up the tree again.

From SPECIMEN DAYS (Autumn Sidebits)

From A SONG OF JOYS

O the farmer's joys!
Ohioan's, Illinoisian's, Wisconsinese', Kanadian's, Iowan's,
    Kansian's, Missourian's, Oregonese' joys!
To rise at peep of day and pass forth nimbly to work,
To plough land in the fall for winter-sown crops,
To plough land in the spring for maize,
To train orchards, to graft the trees, to gather apples in the
    fall.

    This is the hour for strange effects in light and shade —
enough to make a colorist go delirious — long spokes of
molten silver sent horizontally through the trees (now in their
brightest tenderest green,) each leaf and branch of
endless foliage a lit-up miracle, then lying all prone on the
youthful-ripe, interminable grass, and giving the blades
not only aggregate but individual splendor, in ways unknown
to any other hour.

               From SPECIMEN DAYS (Sundown Lights)

The dying sun-spiked sky has a splendor unknown to any other hour.

THOU ORB ALOFT FULL-DAZZLING

Thou orb aloft full-dazzling! thou hot October noon!
Flooding with sheeny light the gray beach sand,
The sibilant near sea with vistas far and foam,
And tawny streaks and shades and spreading blue;
O sun of noon refulgent! my special word to thee.

Hear me illustrious!
Thy lover me, for always I have loved thee,
Even as basking babe, then happy boy alone by some wood
    edge, thy touching-distant beams enough,
Or man matured, or young or old, as now to thee I launch
    my invocation.

(Thou canst not with thy dumbness me deceive,
I know before the fitting man all Nature yields,
Though answering not in words, the skies, trees, hear his
    voice—and thou O sun,
As for thy throes, thy perturbations, sudden breaks and
    shafts of flame gigantic,
I understand them, I know those flames, those perturbations
    well.)

Thou that with fructifying heat and light,
O'er myriad farms, o'er lands and waters North and South,
O'er Mississippi's endless course, o'er Texas' grassy plains,
    Kanada's woods,
O'er all the globe that turns its face to thee shining in space,
Thou that impartially infoldest all, not only continents, seas,
Thou that to grapes and weeds and little wild flowers givest
    so liberally,
Shed, shed thyself on mine and me, with but a fleeting ray
    out of thy million millions,
Strike though these chants.

Nor only launch thy subtle dazzle and thy strength for these,
Prepare the later afternoon of me myself—prepare my
    lengthening shadows,
Prepare my starry nights.

"Give me the juicy autumnal fruit,
ripe and red from the orchard . . ."

Courtesy Wisconsin Department of Natural Resources

Doug Green

74

Wheat fields in Lafayette County, Wisconsin.

From GIVE ME THE SPLENDID SILENT SUN

Give me the splendid silent sun, with all his beams full-
    dazzling;
Give me the juicy autumnal fruit, ripe and red from the
    orchard;
Give me a field where the unmow'd grass grows,
Give me an arbor, give me the trellis'd grape;
Give me fresh corn and wheat—give me serene-moving
    animals, teaching content;
Give me nights perfectly quiet, as on high plateaus west of
    the Mississippi, and I looking up at the stars;
Give me odorous at sunrise a garden of beautiful flowers,
    where I can walk undisturb'd; . . .

Measureless oceans of space are bridged by the noiseless patient spider.

A NOISELESS PATIENT SPIDER

A noiseless patient spider,
I mark'd where on a little promontory it stood isolated,
Mark'd how to explore the vacant vast surrounding,
It launch'd forth filament, filament, filament, out of itself,
Ever unreeling them, ever tirelessly speeding them.

And you O soul where you stand,
Surrounded, detached, in measureless oceans of space,
Ceaselessly musing, venturing, throwing, seeking the
    spheres to connect them,
Till the bridge you will need be form'd, till the ductile anchor
    hold,
Till the gossamer thread you fling catch somewhere, O
    my soul.

From PROUD MUSIC OF THE STORM

Proud music of the storm!
Blast that careers so free, whistling across the prairies!
Strong hum of forest tree-tops! Wind of the mountains!
Personified dim shapes! you hidden orchestras!
You serenades of phantoms, with instruments alert,
Blending, with Nature's rhythms, all the tongues of nations;
You chords left us by vast composers! you choruses!
You formless, free, religious dances! you from the Orient!
You undertone of rivers, roar of pouring cataracts;
You sounds from distant guns, with galloping cavalry!
Echoes of camps, with all the different bugle-calls!
Trooping tumultuous, filling the midnight late, bending
    me powerless,
Entering my lonesome slumber-chamber—Why have you
    seiz'd me?

O vast Rondure, swimming in space, now first it seems
my thought begins to span thee . . .

Oct. 20. A clear, crispy day — dry and breezy air, full
of oxygen. Out of the sane, silent, beauteous miracles
that envelop and fuse me — trees, water, grass, sunlight, and
early frost — the one I am looking at most today is the
sky. It has that delicate, transparent blue, peculiar
to autumn, and the only clouds are little or larger white ones,
giving their still and spiritual motion to the great concave.
All through the earlier day . . . . it keeps a pure, yet
vivid blue. But as noon approaches the color gets lighter,
quite gray for two or three hours — then still paler for
a spell, till sundown — which last I watch dazzling through
the interstices of a knoll of big trees — darts of fire and
a gorgeous show of light yellow, liver color and red, with a
vast silver glaze askant on the water — the transparent
shadows, shafts, sparkle, and vivid colors beyond all the
paintings ever made. . . .

From SPECIMEN DAYS
(The Sky — Days and Nights — Happiness)

THE FIRST DANDELION

Simple and fresh and fair from winter's close emerging,
As if no artifice of fashion, business, politics, had ever been,
Forth from its sunny nook of shelter'd grass — innocent,
    golden, calm as the dawn,
The spring's first dandelion shows its trustful face.

From PASSAGE TO INDIA

O vast Rondure, swimming in space,
Cover'd all over with visible power and beauty,
Alternate light and day and teeming spiritual darkness,
Unspeakable high processions of sun and moon and countless
    stars above,
Below, the manifold grass and waters, animals, mountains,
    trees,
With inscrutable purpose, some hidden prophetic intention,
Now first it seems my thought begins to span thee.

H. Armstrong Roberts

Transparent shadows play along the
silver-glazed waters of sundown.

So here I sit gossiping in the early candle-light of old age — I and my book — casting backward glances over our travel'd road. After completing, as it were, . . . some lengthened ship-voyage, . . . reaching port in a sufficient way through all discomfitures at last . . .

VI
"A Backward Glance
O'er Travel'd Roads"

Perhaps the best of songs heard, or of any and all true love, or life's fairest episodes, or sailors', soldiers' trying scenes on land or sea, is the *résumé* of them, or any of them, long afterwards, looking at the actualities away back past, with all their practical excitations gone. How the soul loves to float amid such reminiscences!

So here I sit gossiping in the early candle-light of old age — I and my book — casting backward glances over our travel'd road. After completing, as it were, the journey — (a varied jaunt of years, with many halts and gaps of intervals — or some lengthen'd ship-voyage, wherein more than once the last hour had apparently arrived, and we seem'd certainly going down — yet reaching port in a sufficient way through all discomfitures at last). . . .

From A BACKWARD GLANCE O'ER TRAVEL'D ROADS

A PAUMANOK PICTURE

Two boats with nets lying off the sea-beach, quite still,
Ten fishermen waiting — they discover a thick school of moss-
    bonkers — they drop the join'd seine-ends in the water,
The boats separate and row off, each on its rounding course
    to the beach, enclosing the mossbonkers,
The net is drawn in by a windlass by those who stop ashore,
Some of the fishermen lounge in their boats, others stand
    ankle-deep in the water, pois'd on strong legs,
The boats partly drawn up, the water slapping against them,
Strew'd on the sand in heaps and windrows, well out from
    the water, the green-back'd spotted mossbonkers.

Gene Ahrens

One lesson from affiliating a tree — perhaps the greatest moral lesson anyhow from earth, rocks, animals, is that same lesson of inherency, of *what is*, without the least regard to what the looker-on (the critic) supposes or says, or whether he likes or dislikes. What worse — what more general malady pervades each and all of us, our literature, education, attitude toward each other, (even toward ourselves,) than a morbid trouble about *seems*, (generally temporarily seems too,) and no trouble at all, or hardly any, about the sane, slow-growing, perennial, real parts of character, books, friendship, marriage — humanity's invisible foundations and hold-together? (As the all-basis, the nerve, the great sympathetic, the plenum within humanity, giving stamp to everything, is necessarily invisible.)

From SPECIMEN DAYS (The Lesson of a Tree)

A Pacific sunset seen at Ecola State Park in Oregon.

One lesson from affiliating a tree — perhaps the greatest moral
lesson anyhow from earth, rocks, animals,
is that same lesson of what is . . .

Doug Green

Whitman's vision of the earth was as boundless as a Kansas prairie.

From SONG OF MYSELF

But each man and each woman of you I lead upon a knoll,
My left hand hooking you round the waist,
My right hand pointing to landscapes of continents and the
    public road.

Not I, not any one else can travel that road for you,
You must travel it for yourself.

It is not far, it is within reach,
Perhaps you have been on it since you were born and did
    not know,
Perhaps it is everywhere on water and on land.

NIGHT ON THE PRAIRIES

Night on the prairies,
The supper is over, the fire on the ground burns low,
The wearied emigrants sleep, wrapt in their blankets;
I walk by myself—I stand and look at the stars, which I
    think now I never realized before.

Now I absorb immortality and peace,
I admire death and test propositions.

82

How plenteous! how spiritual! how résumé!
The same old man and soul—the same old aspirations, and
    the same content.

I was thinking the day most splendid till I saw what the not-
    day exhibited,
I was thinking this globe enough till there sprang out so
    noiseless around me myriads of other globes.

Now while the great thoughts of space and eternity fill me I
    will measure myself by them,
And now touch'd with the lives of other globes arrived as far
    along as those of the earth,
Or waiting to arrive, or pass'd on farther than those of the
    earth,
I henceforth no more ignore them than I ignore my own life,
Or the lives of the earth arrived as far as mine, or waiting
    to arrive.

O I see now that life cannot exhibit all to me, as the day
    cannot,
I see that I am to wait for what will be exhibited by death.

"I was thinking the day most splendid till I saw what the not-day exhibited."

Tom Brockhaus

83

This halcyon scene is Baker Lake in Washington.

Let me not dare, here or anywhere, for my own purposes, or any purposes, to attempt the definition of Poetry, nor answer the question what it is. Like Religion, Love, Nature, while those terms are indispensible, and we all give a sufficiently accurate meaning to them, in my opinion no definition that has ever been made sufficiently encloses the name Poetry; nor can any rule or convention ever so absolutely obtain but some great exception may arise and disregard and overturn it. . . .

From A BACKWARD GLANCE O'ER TRAVEL'D ROADS

HALCYON DAYS

Not from successful love alone,
Nor wealth, nor honor'd middle age, nor victories of politics
    or war;
But as life wanes, and all the turbulent passions calm,
As gorgeous, vapory, silent hues cover the evening sky,
As softness, fulness, rest, suffuse the frame, like fresher,
    balmier air,

Whoever you are! you are he or she for whom
                            the earth is solid and liquid . .

As the days take on a mellower light, and the apple at last
    hangs really finish'd and indolent-ripe on the tree,
Then for the teeming quietest, happiest days of all!
The brooding and blissful halcyon days!

From AN 1855-56 NOTEBOOK TOWARD
THE SECOND EDITION OF LEAVES OF GRASS

I believe whatever happens I shall not forget this earth,
I believe I shall walk and walk among men and women. —
Wherever I go I believe I shall often return.
There are many words and deeds that will happen that will
    allure me,
Where any one thinks of me or wishes me that will allure me,
Where the happy young husband and wife are, and the happy
    old husband and wife are, will allure me.

From A SONG OF THE ROLLING EARTH

Whoever you are! motion and reflection are especially for
    you,
The divine ship sails the divine sea for you.

Whoever you are! you are he or she for whom the earth is
    solid and liquid,
You are he or she for whom the sun and moon hang in the
    sky,
For none more than you are the present and the past,
For none more than you is immortality.

Each man to himself and each woman to herself, is the word
    of the past and present, and the true word of
    immortality;
No one can acquire for another — not one,
Not one can grow for another — not one.

The song is to the singer, and comes back most to him,
The teaching is to the teacher, and comes back most to him,
The murder is to the murderer, and comes back most to him,
The theft is to the thief, and comes back most to him,
The love is to the lover, and comes back most to him,
The gift is to the giver, and comes back most to him — it
    cannot fail,
The oration is to the orator, the acting is to the actor and
    actress not to the audience,
And no man understands any greatness or goodness but his
    own, or the indication of his own.

DAREST THOU NOW O SOUL

Darest thou now O soul,
Walk out with me toward the unknown region,
Where neither ground is for the feet nor any path to follow?

No map there, nor guide,
Nor voice sounding, nor touch of human hand,
Nor face with blooming flesh, nor lips, nor eyes, are in that
    land.

I know it not O soul,
Nor dost thou, all is a blank before us,
All waits undream'd of in that region, that inaccessible land.

Till when the ties loosen,
All but the ties eternal, Time and Space,
Nor darkness, gravitation, sense, nor any bounds bounding
    us.

Then we burst forth, we float,
In Time and Space O soul, prepared for them,
Equal, equipt at last, (O joy! O fruit of all!) them to fulfil O
    soul.

From A SONG OF THE ROLLING EARTH

The earth does not exhibit itself nor refuse to exhibit itself,
    possesses still underneath,
Underneath the ostensible sounds, the august chorus of
    heroes, the wail of slaves,
Persuasions of lovers, curses, gasps of the dying, laughter of
    young people, accents of bargainers,
Underneath these possessing words that never fail.

To her children the words of the eloquent dumb great mother
    never fail,
The true words do not fail, for motion does not fail and
    reflection does not fail,
Also the day and night do not fail, and the voyage we pursue
    does not fail.

Silent, vapory hues cover the evening sky.

Walk out with me toward the unknown region,
Where neither ground is for the feet nor any path to follow . . .

Lud Munchmeyer

Over the tree-tops I float thee a song!
Over the rising and sinking waves — over the myriad fields,
*   and the prairies wide;*
Over the dense-pack'd cities all, and the teeming wharves
*   and ways,*
I float this carol with joy, with joy to thee, O Death!

VII
This Carol with Joy

Haughty this song . . . to span vast realms of time,
Evolution — the cumulative — growths and generations.

L. OF G.'S PURPORT

Not to exclude or demarcate, or pick out evils from their
    formidable masses (even to expose them,)
But add, fuse, complete, extend—and celebrate the immortal
    and the good.

Haughty this song, its words and scope,
To span vast realms of space and time,
Evolution—the cumulative—growths and generations.

Begun in ripen'd youth and steadily pursued,
Wandering, peering, dallying with all—war, peace, day and
    night absorbing,
Never even for one brief hour abandoning my task,
I end it here in sickness, poverty, and old age.

I sing of life, yet mind me well of death:
To-day shadowy Death dogs my steps, my seated shape, and
    has for years—
Draws sometimes close to me, as face to face.

Opposite: This view in the Colorado Rockies
shows the result of countless years of evolution.

Whitman saw youth as full of grace and force.

WHISPERS OF HEAVENLY DEATH

Whispers of heavenly death murmur'd I hear,
Labial gossip of night, sibilant chorals,
Footsteps gently ascending, mystical breezes wafted soft and
    low,
Ripples of unseen rivers, tides of a current flowing, forever
    flowing,
(Or is it the plashing of tears? the measureless waters of
    human tears?)

I see, just see skyward, great cloud-masses,
Mournfully slowly they roll, silently swelling and mixing,
With at times a half-dimm'd sadden'd far-off star,
Appearing and disappearing.

(Some parturition rather, some solemn immortal birth;
On the frontiers to eyes impenetrable,
Some soul is passing over.)

YOUTH, DAY, OLD AGE AND NIGHT

Youth, large, lusty, loving—youth full of grace, force,
    fascination,
Do you know that Old Age may come after you with equal
    grace, force, fascination?

Day full-blown and splendid—day of the immense sun,
    action, ambition, laughter,
The Night follows close with millions of suns, and sleep and
    restoring darkness.

GOOD-BYE MY FANCY!

Good-bye my Fancy!
Farewell dear mate, dear love!
I'm going away, I know not where,
Or to what fortune, or whether I may ever see you again,
So Good-bye my Fancy.

Now for my last—let me look back a moment;
The slower fainter ticking of the clock is in me,
Exit, nightfall, and soon the heart-thud stopping.
Long have we lived, joy'd, caress'd together;
Delightful!—now separation—Good-bye my Fancy.

Yet let me not be too hasty,
Long indeed have we lived, slept, filter'd, become really
    blended into one;
Then if we die we die together, (yes, we'll remain one,)
If we go anywhere we'll go together to meet what happens,
May-be we'll be better off and blither, and learn something,
May-be it is yourself now really ushering me to the true
    songs, (who knows?)
May-be it is you the mortal knob really undoing, turning—
    so now finally,
Good-bye—and hail! my Fancy.

From AS I EBB'D WITH THE OCEAN OF LIFE

As I wend to the shores I know not,
As I list to the dirge, the voices of men and women wreck'd,
As I inhale the impalpable breezes that set in upon me,
As the ocean so mysterious rolls toward me closer and
    closer,
I too but signify at the utmost a little wash'd-up drift,
A few sands and dead leaves to gather,
Gather, and merge myself as part of the sands and drift.

O baffled, balk'd, bent to the very earth,
Oppress'd with myself that I have dared to open my mouth,
Aware now that amid all that blab whose echoes recoil upon
    me I have not once had the least idea who or what I am,
But that before all my arrogant poems the real Me stands
    yet untouch'd, untold, altogether unreach'd,
Withdrawn far, mocking me with mock-congratulatory signs
    and bows,
With peals of distant ironical laughter at every word I have
    written,
Pointing in silence to these songs, and then to the sand
    beneath.

I perceive I have not really understood any thing, not a
    single object, and that no man ever can,
Nature here in sight of the sea taking advantage of me to
    dart upon me and sting me,
Because I have dared to open my mouth to sing at all.

I laugh at what you call dissolution,
And I know the amplitude of time . . .

From WHEN LILACS LAST
IN THE DOOR-YARD BLOOM'D

Then with the knowledge of death as walking one side of me,
And the thought of death close-walking the other side of me,
And I in the middle, as with companions, and as holding
    the hands of companions,
I fled forth to the hiding receiving night, that talks not,
Down to the shores of the water, the path by the swamp
    in the dimness,
To the solemn shadowy cedars, and ghostly pines so still.

And the singer so shy to the rest receiv'd me;
The gray-brown bird I know, receiv'd us comrades three;
And he sang what seem'd the carol of death, and a verse
    for him I love.

From SONG OF MYSELF

I know I am deathless,
I know this orbit of mine cannot be swept by a carpenter's
    compass,
I know I shall not pass like a child's carlacue cut with a
    burnt stick at night. . . .

I exist as I am, that is enough,
If no other in the world be aware I sit content,
And if each and all be aware I sit content.

One world is aware and by far the largest to me, and that is
    myself,
And whether I come to my own to-day or in ten thousand
    or ten million years,
I can cheerfully take it now, or with equal cheerfulness I
    can wait.

My foothold is tenon'd and mortis'd in granite,
I laugh at what you call dissolution,
And I know the amplitude of time.

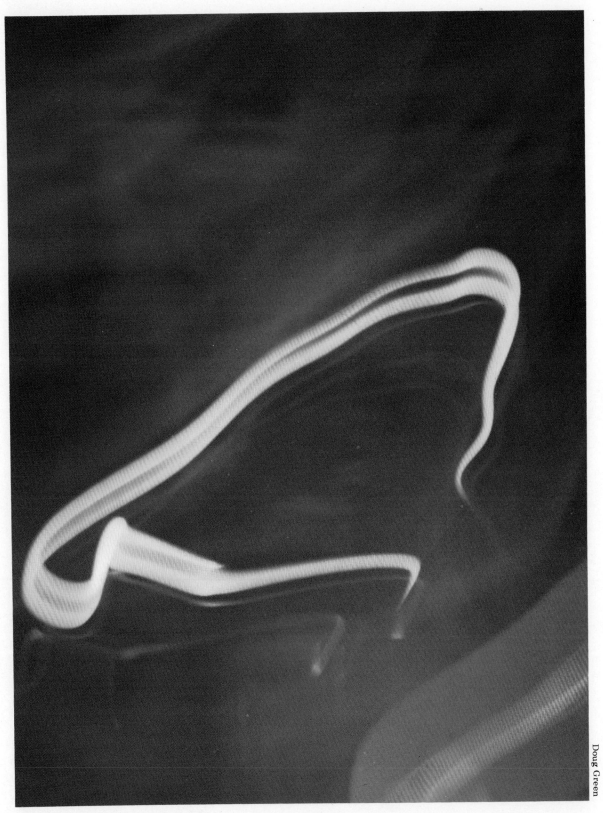

"I exist as I am, that is enough."

Come, lovely and soothing Death . . .

From WHEN LILACS LAST
IN THE DOOR-YARD BLOOM'D

Come, lovely and soothing Death,
Undulate round the world, serenely arriving, arriving,
In the day, in the night, to all, to each,
Sooner or later, delicate Death.

Prais'd be the fathomless universe,
For life and joy, and for objects and knowledge curious;
And for love, sweet love—But praise! praise! praise!
For the sure-enwinding arms of cool-enfolding Death.

Dark Mother, always gliding near, with soft feet,
Have none chanted for thee a chant of fullest welcome?
Then I chant it for thee—I glorify thee above all;
I bring thee a song that when thou must indeed come,
     come unfalteringly.

Approach, strong Deliveress!
When it is so—when thou hast taken them, I joyously sing
     the dead,
Lost in the loving, floating ocean of thee,
Laved in the flood of thy bliss, O Death.

From me to thee glad serenades,
Dances for thee I propose, saluting thee—adornments and
     feastings for thee;
And the sights of the open landscape, and the high-spread
     sky, are fitting,
And life and the fields, and the huge and thoughtful night.

The night, in silence, under many a star;
The ocean shore, and the husky whispering wave, whose
     voice I know;
And the soul turning to thee, O vast and well-veil'd Death,
And the body gratefully nestling close to thee.

Over the tree-tops I float thee a song!
Over the rising and sinking waves—over the myriad fields,
     and the prairies wide;
Over the dense-pack'd cities all, and the teeming wharves
     and ways,
I float this carol with joy, with joy to thee, O Death!

Early settlers are buried beneath these headstones at Harper's Ferry, West Virginia.

GLIDING O'ER ALL

Gliding o'er all, through all,
Through Nature, Time, and Space,
As a ship on the waters advancing,
The voyage of the soul—not life alone,
Death, many deaths I'll sing.

"From the walls of the powerful fortress'd house, / Let me be wafted."

THE LAST INVOCATION

At the last, tenderly,
From the walls of the powerful fortress'd house,
From the clasp of the knitted locks, from the keep of the
     well-closed doors,
Let me be wafted.

Let me glide noiselessly forth;
With the key of softness unlock the locks — with a whisper,
Set ope the doors O soul.

Tenderly — be not impatient,
(Strong is your hold O mortal flesh,
Strong is your hold O love.)